Poetic Secrets

Poetic Secrets

A British Brown Beauty's Perspective

Harmeet Kaur Bharya

Matador
9 Priory Business Park,
Wistow Road, Kibworth Beauchamp,
Leicestershire. LE8 0RX
Tel: 0116 279 2299
Email: books@troubador.co.uk
Web: www.troubador.co.uk/matador
Twitter: @matadorbooks

ISBN 978 1789014 327

British Library Cataloguing in Publication Data.
A catalogue record for this book is available from the British Library.

Printed and bound in Great Britain by 4edge Limited
Typeset in 11pt Minion Pro by Troubador Publishing Ltd, Leicester, UK

Matador is an imprint of Troubador Publishing Ltd

This poetry collection I share with you in the loving memory of my father, Nirmal Singh Thethi, who before he passed on said, 'You should get your poetry published one day.'

I'm here, with Poetic Secrets pouring
out of my heart; to touch the depths
of hearts that cannot be seen,
but only felt.

Contents

About the Author

I was born and raised in the London Borough of Redbridge where I lived with my parents and sister. I started writing poetry at the age of sixteen and went on to study English Literature.

I completed my degree in BSc Computer Science during a challenging time when my father passed on. I went on to become a junior web developer at the University of Hertfordshire where I graduated.

Soon after, I married Mr Right, accepted a new job offer at Book Depository as web developer, became pregnant and bought a house; all within nine months. After the birth of my daughter, I suffered with severe postnatal depression and anxiety for two years. After maternity leave, I returned to work and I was offered the opportunity to train as a project manager when Book Depository became a subsidiary of Amazon. I loved my project management role and thoroughly enjoyed being a part of the Amazon family. I took the decision to leave after five years of employment when I sadly miscarried an early twin pregnancy. Thereafter, I suffered more heartache and severe anxiety that was debilitating; I was unable to leave my home some days and was too scared to drive. My thoughts became morbid, and I started thinking of ways to end my life to escape the misery.

However, with the help of professional and holistic therapies, I am alive and well today to tell the story. I'm currently living in the county of Berkshire with my amazing husband and beautiful daughter. It's now been two and a half years since I started working for my husband's business, Langhams Estate Agents, as Accounts Manager.

The inspiration for my poetry stems from a timeline of sorrow, from some very ugly experiences since the age of eleven, to illness and the loss of loved ones, heartbreak, secondary infertility and miscarriage, anxiety and depression.

Whilst on the road to recovery, I discovered interior design and undertook further education in this field last year, exploring avenues to start a business. Unfortunately, I recently miscarried again after a further two years of trying for a second child. In the midst of my spiritual healing, I revisited all the poetry I had been writing over the years, and began writing more and more each day. I haven't been able to put my pen down since this turning point, and have finally managed to put this collection together. I would best describe myself as a God-fearing soul, and my hobbies include yoga, meditation, interior design, poetry and writing.

Acknowledgements

Above all, the greatest of gratitude I give to my Gurus and God. Everything I am today I owe to my parents: my father, Nirmal Singh Thethi, who encouraged me to write my poetry, and my mother, Surinder Kaur Thethi, who nurtured and supported me through the process. A big thank you to my sister Gurkiran Kaur who kept me going when I doubted myself. I am forever grateful to my little daughter, Harleen Kaur Bharya, who has brought so much inspiration to my life. The biggest thanks go to my husband, Harminder Singh Bharya, my rock, my best friend who has stood by me through this journey. Special thanks to Melanie Valecha, my spiritual healing mentor, who instigated my putting pen to paper after years of dry ink. From the depths of my heart, I thank all those people, too many to name, who inspired my poetry; they taught me some great lessons in life and helped me with my personal growth.

Part 1

Flight, Fight, Freeze

The Panic

When I look into the eyes of the innocent young,
I reminisce over those sweet days before I was stung.

In hindsight, those days, those months were so simple;
It was more often than not that you would see my dimple.

My innocence was stolen and so was my youth,
Ever since, I have felt like I'm trapped in a booth.

A whirlwind of emotions spin inside of me,
As the layers of life deepen like the rough sea.

These thoughts are what make my senses stir,
So when I step outside, the world appears as a blur.

In a vicious circle, round and round it goes:
Panic is here. I failed to fly or fight, so I froze.

It's chaos here in my mind, body and soul,
I'm falling down a distant, dark, damaging hole.

My body is shaking and my mind is numb,
I'm trapped and I don't know where to run.

My soul guides me to a listening ear;
To this professional I let out my fear.

A helping hand, the tools to fight I receive;
I learn that I cannot escape until I grieve.

So whatever sorrow may come my way,
I'm learning to be kinder to myself each day.

Depression

Deeply concealing the emptiness within the heart,

Experiencing nothing but anxiety which never does part,

Pleading to heal the corrupted heart and mind,

Rectifying each situation one comes to find,

Escaping from all that confronts the deep inner weakness,

Separating the tortured heart from loneliness,

Stopping the temperamental mind from further despair,

Intuitively battling the course of bringing pain near,

Often nothing ever stops the tears from the eyes,

Nor ever the empty heart that cries and cries.

Darkness

The roots of my darkness
Are prickly like the cactus.

The heart is sinking,
Whilst my mind is shrinking.

My body is faint and weak,
My words fail to speak.

My mind is anxiously blocked,
My soul is lonely and locked.

Failing to find the right key,
To set my trapped spirit free.

Imprisoned in my own body,
All appears as vague and foggy.

Look into sadness through my eyes,
Peel my layers of onion in disguise.

Burrowed deep here inside,
Is someone you won't recognise.

Fate

I strive to reach for a tranquil happiness,
But I encounter a cloud of emptiness.

All I see is a dark shadow blinding my light;
I wish I could turn the wrong into right.

Always been there to lend a shoulder to cry on,
Now the need is here, searching for those who have gone.

Instead of walking happily, I walk alone;
Like the sound of a violin, I hear my heart moan.

All I can do tirelessly is wait,
Until my impatient wait leads me to fate.

Lowest Point

Another day where assumptions inevitably lay,
Another day where underestimations overstay.

There is no understanding of the state of mind,
No idea of the feelings that hide deep inside.

No support to heal the crushed heart and broken trust,
It is not a feeling that can be wiped away like dust.

It is a layer within the soul thick and concealed;
The thicker the layer becomes, the less is revealed.

Each minute of outrage anticipates a long walk away,
Away from the darkness to find a shining ray.

There is no way out, just a trapped being,
No freedom of decision, life has no meaning.

Not even a slight bit of control,
Just the feeling of playing a role.

Great Loss

Ruminations of you overshadow reality,
The congested mind anticipates tranquility.

The whisper of your voice is obscured by the daylight's essence,
The remorse beat plays until its rhythm becomes immense.

The sorrow of your absence becomes unbearable,
That something felt, heard and seen only remains memorable.

That tear makes a journey through the mirrors of my heart,
The tenderness is still recreating even whilst we are apart.

Though I'm awake, I see you in my sleep, I see you in my dream,
Though it seems misty, I see a bright shining beam.

The flames I feel, the thoughts I think, the beats that burn,
Because this is all I have; heartfelt memories that churn.

The Mood

It reflects the cloudy moods in the sky,
The whistling wind hits and forces a tear in the eye.

The trees stir emotions from side to side,
The narrow path between them becomes a guide.

Such spacious grounds, yet such narrow paths,
Never-ending as it lasts, lasts and lasts.

The silence whispers tearfully a rainy downpour,
Until it loses the will to cry any more.

Striving to forbid further agony,
Walking no further than that oak of not many.

When it reaches a motion of sensitivity,
It brings nothing but inferior intensity.

One by one, each raindrop begins to mingle,
With that tear in the eye that remains single.

Confusion

Why do the corners of my mind stand confused,
Like a second-hand feeling of having being so used.

This feeling blocks the corners of the mind,
Not knowing whether to leave it all behind.

Sending impulses of confusion in all directions,
Losing the ability with all inner connections.

Leaving no way out,
All except two sides of doubt.

If only I could find the answers and see,
Of what the truth may be.

But all I find are tears of misery,
The times when we both said sorry.

Why do I feel so trapped,
In cotton wool was I wrapped.

What should I do, what should I say,
To make this confusion go away.

Truth Be Told

Once upon a time when I was young,
When I hadn't learnt to use my tongue,

Truth be told, school just wasn't any fun,
I was picked on and had nowhere to run.

Just because my skin was brown,
And I went to school in a white town

They sneered at my long black hair,
Again and again each day as a dare.

Educate your mind, I would think,
Too afraid to kick up a stink.

I wish I knew then what I know now,
To make it all go away somehow.

The daggers went deeper than deep,
And the digs were cheaper than cheap.

But I'm here intact with my dignity,
And head held high with humility.

A great lesson it was they taught me,
How to walk on British land in a saree.

Emptiness

When troubles leave the mind, one smiles,
However, this only lasts the briefest while.

The mind is always occupied with unhappiness,
Even the smallest of things stir an angriness.

The feeling is like a dark following shadow,
A bit like walking alone through a meadow.

The mind is always saddened and confused,
Nothing said or done makes one feel amused.

The heart is filled with loneliness and despair,
Making each and every day harder to bear.

The sleepless nights and unwanted pain,
Ravel on and on and drive one insane.

There comes a time when one can take no more,
One begins wondering what life is worth living for.

Yearning within the heart and soul to break free,
But, there is too much emptiness for this to be.

The heart cries and cries each second that goes by,
Wanting to know why, why, why.

Strangled Breath

A tightness took my breath away,
Not in the usual positive way;

With no breath to speak,
An inhalation so weak,

An internal furry wheeze
Strangling the life out of me.

Drifting into a manic mind,
Leaving all sanity behind,

The gift to breathe easily or at all
Is taken for granted like it's so small.

With each breath that comes from above,
Inhale and exhale with gratitude and love.

When I'm relieved of my strangled state,
I become in awe of every breath I take.

Anxious Mind

Despair and doubt,
Why do they shout.

It's dizzy here inside,
On a never-ending ride.

What a fuzzy mind,
Thoughts all misaligned.

I just want to escape,
Block this voice with tape.

This is complete misery,
Always feeling so jittery.

With myself I do fight,
Strangling myself so tight.

How do I become free,
In place with my dignity.

If only you could see,
All the debris inside of me.

Bittersweet Life

It's a bittersweet life I live,
I've given all I have to give.

I am fed and watered in a warm home,
Yet I feel a pain in every single bone.

I'm blessed with enough,
Yet I'm finding it so tough.

No one hears my silent whisper,
Except only my beloved mister.

Yet I'm still alive, but I'm almost dead inside,
Crying for help to stop this roller coaster ride.

In a vicious circle, round and round I spin,
The pain is pricking me like a sharp pin.

How shallow could my thoughts be,
How did I blind myself so I cannot see.

Self-destructing and an unhappy me,
I have to love myself; this is my key.

I tell myself it's not too late to start again,
The time has come to find my Zen.

Mind, Body and Soul

As my mind collapsed, so did my body and soul;
I kept collapsing into the roots of a dark hole.
My mind became as heavy as my body,
My body as light as the soul within me.
Mind, body and soul all turned inside out,
With each collapse planting a seed of doubt.
Once each began to connect and mingle,
The power grew greater than when single.

The Indian Bride

The shy Indian bride dressed in red,
Begins a new journey the day she is wed.

Leaving her home to fulfil another,
Embracing a new family, leaving her mother.

What a surreal feeling to feel,
Like a dream but amazingly real.

Open-heartedly transitioning each day,
Making sure she's not in anyone's way.

Here they do all follow the tradition,
She feels so compelled to just listen.

Such powerful and influential voices,
Oblivious to any of her said choices.

Consciously feeling a little inferior,
Each passing day serving her superior.

She's such a small fish in such a big sea,
Trying to be the best version she can be.

Treading on eggshells as the days go by,
Why is she ignored every time she does try.

Her future has started looking so bleak,
Making her feel so miserable and weak.

She genuinely longed to be part of them all,
Was she taken for granted for being so small

She persevered with all her strength,
Despite the atmosphere being so intense.

Even when she offered her insight,
It was as if only they could be right.

She felt belittled and entirely alone,
It just didn't feel like her home.

Foolishly, she let most things slide,
Bottled them up on the inside.

She couldn't contend with all this weight,
Drowning in poison and so much hate.

It was crystal clear she had to move on,
When she began to feel like a black swan.

Part 2

Childless with Child

Monthlies

When I was just eleven years old,
There was so much I hadn't been told.

Of the redness that would leak,
At first, it just made me shriek.

To my mother I then complained,
Why were my smalls bloodstained;

Was I dying so young and pretty,
All was explained in a voice of pity.

A life-changing moment it did bring,
Transpiring now to a monthly thing.

Now I was not so little and sweet,
My older self I was imposed to meet.

Motherhood

Babies aren't born easy,
In your tummy you feel queasy.

The excitement comes first,
Followed by increasing thirst.

The heightened smell,
Almost makes you yell.

From a dancing mood,
Swiftly to a tone so rude.

With the growing jelly in the belly,
The last few days immersed in telly,

Finally arrives your bundle of joy,
Revealing whether it's a girl or boy.

The sleepless days and nights,
The inner crying fights.

There's just no time to stop,
For a quick moment to change your top.

By now you've transformed into a robot,
You're feeling like you've lost the plot.

The million dirty nappies and cries for milk,
Life is all cotton, gone are the days of silk.

Of course they are beautiful and sweet,
That teeny nose and the cutest little feet.

But it's a twenty-four-hour role,
You are constantly on patrol.

Be careful, it can really drain you out,
When there is no other grown-up about.

Remember, there could be no job more rewarding,
When you wake up to their smile every morning.

Make the most of your little one,
One day they will not be so young.

Like me, you'll wake up one day,
Wondering how quickly those days went away.

Take it from me, these moments don't last forever,
My little one is now six, gone are those days now I treasure.

Don't forget to cut yourself some slack,
And give yourself a pat on the back.

You are doing a truly great job.

Friend

She was my life jacket when I became a mum,
Afraid to leave my home, to me she'd come.

She listened to my tears and hugged my pain,
Picked up broken parts of me, sheltered me in rain.

She held my hand on the journey out,
With my baby when there was no other about.

She'd give a listening ear when I was moping,
Make me tea in my own home when I wasn't coping.

In troubled times she was my only friend,
Shadowing me until the very end.

Heartbeat

When I see on the screen,
The tiny heartbeat of my bean

Fluttering away so effortlessly,
How mesmerising it feels to see

This little life growing inside of me,
Wondering whether you're a he or she.

We had made so many plans for you,
Pretty pictures in my mind I drew.

Sadly, we couldn't meet,
To share a life so sweet.

You will always be in my heart,
Even though we are now apart.

Infertility

Everywhere I go and whoever I see,
They are always asking me.

Are you having another one they ask,
As if it were just a simple task.

Little do they know how I've tried and failed,
When I lost my angels, how I wailed.

Of course, I crave for more than one,
Another one to call me Mum.

It's hard enough getting through each day,
Without listening to what they have to say.

I want the world, just to let me be,
From my heart I make this plea.

Please don't pry into my life,
Don't dig into me with your knife.

So hear me now, no more prying,
Believe me that I am already trying.

Love and patience I wish to receive,
Take this pressure off whilst I conceive.

Childless Child

When I see that glimmer of hope in her eye,
It weakens my strength and makes me cry.

She is such a gentle, kind soul,
Who needs a tiny angel to make her whole.

She longs for a soft little hand to hold,
Someone to cuddle when the days are cold.

If only I could make her dream come true,
If only those tiny angels grew.

I still believe the day will come,
That we will be blessed with another one.

To love and to cherish forever more,
To banish the moments we felt so sore.

I wish upon that star every night,
Whilst embracing my little one so tight.

May we be blessed with those tiny toes,
And wave goodbye to all our woes.

Come to Me, Little One

I'm wishing upon a star,
I'm wondering where you are.

I long for you every day,
I imagine you here as I lay.

Holding you in my arms,
As you show me all your charms.

A teeny tiny button nose,
Cheeks the colour of a rose.

That soft and supple skin,
That precious little chin.

Those innocent little eyes,
That tender voice that cries.

I'm waiting here for you to appear,
So I can whisper lullabies in your ear.

Come to me, my sweet little one,
Come and meet your loving mum.

Sweet, Little and Innocent

This precious little angel blessed from above,
Makes life so beautiful and fills us with love.

The beauty of her smile and twinkly eyes,
I love all of her even when she cries.

Her chuckles are charming when we speak,
She's been my strength when I've felt weak.

I'm mesmerised even when she sleeps,
When I don't see her, I miss her heaps.

She brings to my life so much meaning,
Ever since she arrived, I began healing.

In my heart she is like one of my own,
A special soul she is, I've always known.

Snow White

As the sprinkles of white coated the earth,
Negating winter blues with a needed new birth.

Warming the winter's heart chambers,
Melting tired icicles into heated rivers.

Walking hand in hand with her little sweet pea,
Engrossed in her as she paced towards an iced tree.

Snowflakes glistened on her voluminous lashes,
As she gazed at the white dust on the branches.

Her eyes suddenly so radiant and bright,
Looking as beautiful as the snow white.

Part 3

Mindful Healing

Healing Organs

There's a wind blowing through me,
Whistling to each organ of wonder,
Trapping the treacherous energy
From each scrunched up tissue,
Howling at the murmur of a leaky valve
To soften the tone of my inner peace,
Nipping my goose bumps in their buds,
Restoring balance as it circulates continually.

Patience

Patience is a virtue, they say,
His perfect timing blows me away.

When the weight of the wait is lifted,
When a chance for change is gifted.

Discovering a world so brightened,
Suddenly, the loud load is lightened.

The tomorrows are now exciting,
Morbid chapters I'm now rewriting.

Though the taste of pain has brought me here,
The wait was worth it, and every sore tear.

Proud Scar

Don't ever be ashamed to reveal the scar,
Of tough days that promoted you to where you are.

Wear it like a crown on your head,
To celebrate all the days that you bled.

Thank the deepest of your pains,
For the lessons on changing lanes.

Kiss the feet of those who turned a blind eye,
Their absence taught you how to stand high.

Without the hurdles positioned in your way,
There would be no way to be who you are today.

Thirty-Five

On this day I was given the gift of life,
I'm living the dream of being a mum and wife.

Counting my blessings, I must confess,
With the greatest of gratitude, I express.

For the highs and lows that came my way,
Have made me the woman I am today.

So humbly, I thank my Guru, my creator,
There could be no love that is greater.

Onwards and Upwards

I'm a little better now,
I'm here to show you how.

A step at a time, I took a leap of faith,
Believing in myself made me feel so safe.

I knew when it was time to ask,
To help myself dispose of my mask.

Days and months of recovery,
To erase the years of misery.

I opened my mind to a new avenue,
Cleansed all demons stuck like glue.

All my sorrows began shrinking,
When I explored new ways of thinking.

Positive thoughts became my friend,
It was a new beginning, not the end.

I looked inside of myself and found
The answers to turn my life around.

Everything I needed was always there,
I learnt to love myself and ease my fear.

Words of Art

Just a little patience is all I need,
A little motivation to plant a new seed.

Giving myself a little self-compassion,
Making self-healing my new fashion.

Taking pieces of my wounded heart,
To create these beautiful words of art.

Turning the flavours of my adversities,
Into new and meaningful opportunities.

My heartaches are my newly founded strength,
I'm taking the beauty of this to a new length.

It's giving me new reason to grow upon,
It's given me the will I needed to carry on.

No longer do I conceal when I'm feeling blue,
I've sailed the rough seas, and so can you.

Lifting Others

Nothing is more beautiful,
And truly so delightful

Than a smile that's struggled through tears,
And fought through a timeline of fears.

Striving to stand out from the crowd,
Being a rainbow in someone's cloud.

We lift ourselves by lifting others,
Piercing through blackness to find radiant colours.

Living our lives to impress the creator,
Because there is nothing and no one greater.

Seasons

Whilst the seasons are stalled and still,
Embrace the fierceness of the chalky chill.

Despite the spring in your step being lost,
Before long, the sun will melt your frost.

Use the fire within to warm your bitter mind,
Fill it with a garden full of flowers all entwined.

It doesn't have to be all cloudy skies and rain,
Drift out of this clammy, bewildering chain.

Seek a season within that melts your heart,
An imperishable rosy strength that never departs.

Sunny Again

When the sun begins smiling again,
Diffusing rays through every vein,

Warming the inner curled chambers,
Releasing a rainbow of vibrant vapours,

The freshness of the frisky air
Shines brightly with a silky stare,

Lighting a candle deep within,
Arousing a summer to begin.

Slow and Steady Wins the Race

Look inside your heart and you will find
The answers you need to cleanse your mind.

When you can't find the will to carry on,
When you're alone and feeling withdrawn.

You can find the strength to make it ease,
You can kneel down and pray on your knees.

Put one foot in front of the other,
Travel the darkness to find colour.

Through the inner workings of your soul,
You will find the power to make you whole.

It isn't pretend and this isn't the end,
It's just a blip you can slowly mend.

There's not a shadow of doubt,
How great it feels to let it all out.

How amazing does it feel,
To know that all of this can heal.

Prince

Precious Prince is a healer,
Bringing love to the feeler.

The softness of his fur,
The comfort of his purr.

His tenacious ways
Bring exciting days.

He has a sense of soul,
He knows how to console.

He has a way of expressing love,
Different to the way a human does.

He brings such a difference,
When others show ignorance.

Even without the voice to speak,
He always uplifts me when I'm weak.

New Interior

When I looked into my frayed interior,
It dawned on me, it needed new criteria

To redefine those dulled colours,
Put up new and beautiful shiny mirrors,

Redress the torn lining where the soul lives,
Uncover each compartment with open motives;

A transition so delightful and warm,
An ambience so unlike the norm.

Now when I look inside my interior,
It faithfully reflects my exterior.

A Better Me

Take a look at me now; I filled my empty space,
Leaving behind the days my heart would race.

Found a new meaning to my lonely name,
Fought through the sorrow and the pain.

Showing my shuddering shadows to the door,
Entertaining no space for this agony no more.

Life is now only beautiful and sweet,
Only tastes of kindness I shall greet.

With every leap of faith I take,
A soul-lifting impact it does make.

Beautiful Nature

The mesmerised mind is lost at sea,
Feet in the sand, waves to the knee.

A breath of fresh air and sunny glaze,
Clear blue skies, no more rainy days.

The softness of the gentle breeze,
A moment to stop, a moment to seize.

The synergy of the sun, the sea and the sand,
Is a beauty beyond any other dreamland.

There is no other in my heartspace,
When I close my eyes I visit this place.

Inner Light

My inner light has given me the gift to write,
Words are flowing from morning through night.

Messages speaking from the inner voice,
Some days, creating a profound noise.

The deeper mirrors of emotion are open,
Barriers of all taboo truths are broken.

Exposing a naked, transparent soul,
To spread a message and to console.

Sweet Tongue

Sometimes you have to pick up the crumbs
Of spilt words from sour tongues.

Striking at the speed of a train on a track,
Tainted words can't be swallowed back.

Always think with a tidy mind
Of words that are clean and kind.

Nothing is to be gained from being bitter,
So decorate your words with lots of glitter.

Dive deep into the river of your soul,
To find the part of you your ego stole.

A Somebody

Be that special somebody,
Who makes each and everybody,
Feel like they are a somebody.

With the innocence in your soul,
Be the closing to someone's hole.

Find the compassion in your heart,
To mend those who have fallen apart.

With humble acts of kindness,
Be the light in someone's darkness.

Be that special somebody,
Who makes each and everybody,
Feel like they are a somebody.

Soul Beauty

Believe something beautiful is about to happen.
This is now my newly found weapon.

Believe in your blessed ability,
Live life with great humility.

When life has taken its toll,
The power is within to make you whole.

There is a hidden beauty in your soul,
A gifted guidance towards your goal.

Guru

Today he came and spoke to me,
Magnifying my sight to help me see.

Through the wisdom of your voice,
He challenged my clumsy choice.

With obscure greatness, he made himself seen,
Channelling me back to my vivid dream.

So eloquently clarifying my path,
Which I thought was of the past.

He crystalised my faith so beautifully,
That a power above is taking care of me.

Divine Gate

To be half the person he wants one to be,
One must cleanse the soul and set it free.

To walk on the path of the truth,
As pure as a child with a milk tooth.

To have no fear and no hate,
Opening a pathway to the divine gate.

To go beyond the illusions of life,
Washing away all sin and distancing strife.

To quench the hunger for a grace so true,
Switch on the internal light one never knew.

Treasured Beauties

You can climb mountains so high,
Reach for the stars in the twilight sky.

Discover the beauty in all things so true,
So many there are, but just to name a few:

The twittering tweets of the magpie,
The genius journey of the butterfly.

The timeless tallness of the trees,
The healing honey from the bees.

The sweet scent from the jasmine,
The travelled talent of the dolphin.

Inhale the magic in the moment of time,
Traits of these treasures will help you climb.

Part 4

Love Actually

Forever Love

I thought you were special the moment we met,
That surely you were someone I would never forget.

Then we fell in love and I knew we could share
The happiest life together of two people anywhere.

You share with me in every way
A love that flowers day by day.

You are charming and disarming,
So desirable and true.

You inspire me and impress me,
And that's why I love you.

My love for you will always stay
As passionate as it is today.

And even when we are far apart,
The love does not fade within my heart.

For you, my heart does exhilarate,
My senses stir, my passions burn.

Spoken words leave an imprint on my heart,
You made my head turn from the very start.

I want you to hold me in your arms
And partake in all of my charms.

I want to love you openly,
So all my passions can be free.

I want to hear your sighs
And gaze into the deep pools of your dreamy eyes.

My love for you is a burning flame of fire,
Which I hope you will forever desire.

Patient Love

Every second, every minute, every hour we are apart,
Is a burning sensation in the corners of my heart.

Yet very patiently I wait for when I next see that smile,
That precious smile that captured me from a mile.

If only you knew how true these words were,
If only you could hear these senses stir.

Only then so peacefully could you walk beside me,
Only then so passionately could you let our love be.

Your heart would never look back,
There would be nothing that you would lack.

I only wish that you could see what I see,
Every second, every minute, every hour you are with me.

Why?

You left me and my heart does ache,
As if you pierced it with a stake.

How could you break my heart this way,
How could you throw my love away.

How could you turn your back on me,
How could your thoughts so shallow be

And make my heart in anguish cry,
For having fallen for a lie.

What made you leave without regret,
Was it boredom or was it debt.

Now endlessly, I meet each day,
My spirit dulled, in hues of grey.

My future now is so unclear,
For loneliness is what I fear.

Please torture me no more, I plead,
Come back to me, it's you I need.

Sacred Wish

In unfortunate times it hurts to let go,
When a feeling seeps through, don't let it grow.

A feeling of all your hopes and dreams washed away,
Letting go of this forsaken love seems like the only way.

It hurts so much when memories spin in the mind,
It makes me relive the days I am leaving behind.

Left with a wonder of what I will miss,
And whether I will be granted my sacred wish.

Just feels like my life has fallen apart,
Waiting for that someone to find the key to my heart.

Supported

You travelled to lift me when I was down,
You wiped my tears and threw away my frown.

You flew down like an angel from the sky,
You gave back my life and then just walked on by.

Why was it that you could not stay,
Do you think of me, like I think of you as I lay.

Wondering if you're concealing feelings that remain,
Wondering if you'll ever return and say my name.

Reflecting on what I truly had,
Thinking back just makes me sad.

Yearning to hear your voice and see your smile,
To look into your eyes, if only for a little while.

I'd give my all to spend one more moment with you,
To open my heart and say all the things I wanted to.

Now they shall remain concealed inside,
Unless you return to be by my side.

Wonder

Each moment forward feels like two steps back,
Maybe it is due to the support that I lack.

It is effortless to say you are going to walk away,
But that love, that hope, remains in my heart each day.

Although someone has treated you bad,
It doesn't wipe the feelings you had.

It may seem wise to let go,
Not to let your wounds show.

To return the pain they inflicted on you,
Though true love doesn't allow one to do.

Sending a true love some pain,
Is not the answer to bring you gain.

Such confusion makes me wonder hopelessly,
Sleepless nights and empty days, living so restlessly.

Will I ever find the key to my answer,
Before my feelings become tenser.

Love Plant

It's not by choice to be in love with you,
Not a clue in sight of what to do.

With great courage I try
To tamper my helpless cry.

This love plant is thriving in every way
Despite me watering it less each day.

Why is it that you have hurt me so much,
Why do I still long to feel your touch.

Without you, I'm struggling to survive,
I need you to keep me alive.

Words

Never a feeling that's surfaced before,
A piece of my heart you played with and tore.

It hurts so much to hear from you,
Of something that is so untrue.

The words you've spoken have pierced my heart,
The bitter voice is only driving us apart.

Hand on my heart, I have never lied,
The truth I have never tried to hide.

It may take some time for my heart to fill,
For every tear that you made me spill.

It's the way that words have hurt,
You've taught me and I have learnt.

A soul like mine you will never find,
You know inside of your heart and mind.

Deception

The mind is in the space of the dark,
Losing all sense and my usual spark.

What could make one do such a thing,
Only horrible pain it does bring.

A feeling of being so led on,
A sense of being so withdrawn.

No matter what you do or say,
My love beats each and every day.

You've become the token of this love,
Which surely comes from the one above.

I've expressed the true love I feel,
These emotions you cannot steal.

Fragments

Sieve the mind of what I'm going through,
To find the fragments of what is true.

Detain the pieces that look so fine,
To find a piece of you that became mine.

Maybe you choose to turn a blind eye,
Just to let my love walk by.

I think of you here as I lay,
The love is too deep to step away.

Why make promises you cannot keep,
To shatter the dream of someone so weak.

I cannot suppress my feelings, I confess,
I know you do not feel the love I possess.

Why do you choose not to hear me,
Why do you not let me say what needs to be.

Anticipation

Reuniting with you once again is my dream,
If only I could express how much you mean.

Longing to feel your touch once again,
Run to me and whisper when.

Anticipating what we had before,
Come and open my heart's door.

Show me that you still care,
A love like mine is so very rare.

Nothing can tear my love apart,
Everything you do touches my heart.

Kiss me and take my breath away,
Accept my love and make my day.

Loving you always I think you know,
So come back to me and never go.

An Imprint

Love is blind,
Love is difficult to find.

It begins like a spark,
And remains like a mark.

Love is an imprint left in one's heart,
Nothing can pull this imprint apart.

Thoughts just do not leave the mind,
Until one day when one does find

The passion within this sacred imprint,
That blows to the mind a subtle hint.

The decision then one should make,
A step further, this imprint one should take.

Admiration

May all your hopes and dreams come true,
May the passion between us never feel blue.

To be with you is my dream,
Just a passerby I may seem.

My emotions I wish to declare,
Holding me back is my fear.

My love for you does always burn,
My thoughts to you do turn.

I wish one day it will be so much more,
It's everything about you that I adore.

Just When

Just when I thought love would never be a part of me,
That's when you came along and sprinkled some happiness.

Just when I thought I'd never find the love I'd been seeking,
That's when you came along to open the door to my heart.

Just when I thought I was going to fall,
That's when you came along to catch me before I fell.

Just when I thought I was going to walk alone,
That's when you came along and held my hand.

Just when I thought life was going to be a lonely day,
That's when you came along and filled my heart.

Just when I thought I could never love again,
That's when you came along and found the key to my heart.

Sweet Nothings

When a piece of you became mine,
I decorated it in chocolatey rich
With pieces of my honeycomb,
A recipe for our melting moments,
With sprinkles of your sweet icing
Dusting over my imperfections.
Thank you for being so golden delicious,
My cherry on top of the hundreds and thousands.

Flattery

Your loving affections spell the difference between happiness and despair,
Your caress is a delight to experience and so uniquely rare.

Your devotion, respect and loyalty are the substance of my happiness,
Your love and affection have healed my sore wounds and emptied my sadness.

Your sustaining love makes the gloomy reality of this world bearable,
Your sweet ways and caress act like a magnet which is so irresistible.

Your articulate manner and softly spoken words are music to my ears,
Your tender love is truly inspiring which I will cherish for endless years.

When You Believe

When you are sitting in the darkest solitude at night,
Imagining the days that were shining bright

Those days seem so far away melting in the sun,
Those days seem to have ended just as they begun.

My reminiscing tells me that I am drowned in you,
And I cannot find the strength to pull through.

I assumed you would always be there,
I thought you would always care.

But who knows what miracles you can achieve,
When you just believe.